For Your Wedding

F L O W E R S

For Your Wedding

FLOWERS

Tracy Guth

Principal Photography by Lyn Hughes

FRIEDMAN/FAIRFAX
PUBLISHERS

A FRIEDMAN/FAIRFAX BOOK

Library of Congress Cataloging-in-Publication Data available upon request.

ISBN 1-56799-810-0

Editor: Ann Kirby
Art Director: Jeff Batzli
Designer: Stephanie Bart-Horvath
Photography Editor: Wendy Missan
Production Manager: Ingrid McNamara

Color separations by Colourscan Overseas Co Pte Ltd
Printed in Hong Kong by C&C Offset Printing Co. Ltd.

1 3 5 7 9 10 8 6 4 2

For bulk purchases and special sales, please contact:
Friedman/Fairfax Publishers
Attention: Sales Department
15 West 26th Street
New York, New York 10010
212/685-6610   FAX 212/685-1307

Visit our website:
www.metrobooks.com

Front cover photograph: ©Lyn Hughes

CONTENTS

INTRODUCTION

Love is a canvas furnished by Nature and embroidered by imagination.
—Voltaire

From an elaborate, traditional affair to a New Age interpretation or even a quick jaunt down to city hall, no wedding would be the same without flowers. The tremendous variety of flower types and arrangement styles enable every bride and groom to find a beautiful, unique, and personal way to incorporate florals into their attire, accessories, and decor.

Flowers are a crucial element of wedding style, whether you hire a floral designer to transform your ceremony and reception spaces into magical gardens or choose to create your own bouquets and centerpieces with blooms from the farmer's market the same morning. You'll likely begin considering your flowers soon after you've chosen your wedding location and your dress. Some brides even choose their wedding date based on when their favorite flowers are in season.

Even though flowers are short-lived, they make powerful keepsakes. Of the five senses, the nose has the best "memory" and the greatest power in evoking recollections. For years to come, the scent of the flowers you wore on your wedding day will bring on vivid memories of the event.

Throughout the ages, herbs and flowering plants have been an integral part of the wedding celebration, signifying bounty and fidelity. In ancient Rome, both bride and groom wore garlands of wheat, rye, and oats to ensure fertility. The pungent smell of herbs was believed to ward off evil spirits; in fact, brides and their attendants originally carried bunches of herbs and spices to drive off demons trying to curse the couple on their wedding day. Elizabethan brides carried garlic and chives for that purpose, but they also included mint and marigold as aphrodisiacs, parsley for fertility, and basil for luck. The Greeks liked ivy for weddings; for them, it represented friendship, love, and marriage.

Orange blossoms have long been connected to weddings, as well; because their evergreen trees bloom and bear fruit at the same time, they symbolize everlasting fulfillment and happiness. It's even said that Juno, the Roman goddess of marriage, received orange blossoms from Jupiter on their momentous wedding day. Famous brides from Queen Victoria to Jacqueline Onassis wore or carried orange blossoms as part of their bridal attire.

In the Middle Ages, brides and their attendants started wearing flowers in their hair. Rosemary, symbolizing remembrance, was a bouquet mainstay. Myrtle was important as far back as ancient Greece, where it was associated with Aphrodite, the goddess of love, and it became popular again in early Victorian times, representing

the constancy of the lovers' emotion. The Victorian era (1837–1901) also heralded the appearance of the round, compact nosegay and smaller posy bouquets, as well as tussie-mussies, tiny clutches of flowers carried in conical silver holders.

The Victorians took things to a whole new level by carefully documenting the meaning of each bloom so that the bouquets and flowers they gave to intimates at a variety of social events—not just weddings—would be infused with secret meaning. They sometimes even selected flowers according to the letters of names,

RICHLY COLORED ROSES ARE ATTACHED TO A HEADBAND TO CREATE A DRAMATIC HEADPIECE FOR THE BRIDE. SUCH VIVID COLORS CAN CREATE A FABULOUS CONTRAST TO THE PURE WHITE OF HER WEDDING GOWN. THIS KIND OF ORNAMENT IS ALSO PERFECT FOR FLOWER GIRLS.

creating a bouquet that spelled something important; for example, if your husband-to-be's first name was Todd, you might group tulips, orchids, daisies, and daffodils to spell it out. *The Language of Flowers*, first published in the nineteenth century, was considered the final word on floral connotations and became an important reference for much of the century.

The meanings of different flowers may move you to include them in your celebration. Here are some of the most popular wedding blooms and what they represent. The colors you choose may affect significance, and some shades even have bad connotations, so if you're superstitious, ask your florist!

DIFFERENT FLOWERS IN THE SAME COLOR FAMILY MAKE FOR A VIVID YET UNDERSTATED BOUQUET. HERE, A NOSEGAY OF PINK, LAVENDER, AND ROSE CREATES A SIMPLE BUT FRAGRANT AND COLORFUL BOUQUET.

Amaryllis: *Beauty, pride*

Anemone: *Expectation, anticipation*

Baby's breath: *Innocence, pure heart*

Blue violet: *Faithfulness*

Calla lily: *Magnificent beauty*

Camellia: *Luck, contentment*

Carnation: *Fidelity, love*

Chrysanthemum (mum): *Abundance, constancy, truth, hope*

Crocus: *Joy*

Daffodil: *Regard, devotion*

Daisy: *Innocence, faith*

Fern: *Sincerity*

Forget-me-not: *Remembrance, constancy*

Freesia: *Innocence*

Gardenia: *Purity, joy*

Gerbera daisy: *Beauty*

Gladiola: *Generosity*

Honeysuckle: *Affection, devotion*

Hyacinth: *Constancy, play, loveliness*

Hydrangea: *Understanding*

Iris: *Faith, wisdom, passion*

Ivy: *Fidelity, wedded love*

Lilac: *First feelings of love or first love, innocence*

Lily of the valley: *Happiness*

Magnolia: *Love of nature*

Orange blossom: *Eternal love, fertility*

Orchid: *Love, beauty*

Peony: *Shyness, happy marriage*

Poppy: *Pleasure, success*

Rose: *Love, joy, beauty; red and white together mean unity; pink signifies grace and gentility; yellow stands for joy and passion; coral indicates desire*

Stephanotis: *Happiness in marriage, desire*

Stock: *Bonds of affection*

Sunflower: *Adoration*

Sweet pea: *Bliss*

Tulip: *Perfect love, passion*

White lily: *Purity, gaiety, sweetness*

MINIATURE WHITE ROSES
CREATE A STUNNING BRIDAL
PURSE WITH ADDED DIMENSION.
THIS SIMPLE, UNADORNED
GOWN IS THE PERFECT BACK-
DROP FOR AN EVENING BAG
SO SUPREMELY SPECIAL AND
ORNATE. THE SATIN BOW
ECHOES THE FABRIC OF
THE DRESS.

The Victorians also assigned each month of the year its own flower, and wearing or carrying the right bloom for your wedding date was believed to bring luck:

January: *Snowdrop*	July: *Larkspur*
February: *Primrose*	August: *Poppy*
March: *Jonquil*	September: *Morning glory*
April: *Sweet pea*	October: *Cosmos*
May: *Lily of the valley*	November: *Chrysanthemum*
June: *Rose*	December: *Holly*

Traditionally, wedding flowers were all white—roses, lilies, freesia, stephanotis, gardenias, orange blossoms, orchids—but color gradually seeped into bouquets and arrangements. Modern weddings offer floral representations of all the colors of the rainbow and more, from vivid yellows and bright pinks to deep purples and tangy citrus shades.

Try to book the services of a florist at least six months before your wedding; a year is not too early for some in-demand professionals. You'll meet again closer to the date (about three months before) to finalize your floral decisions and place an order. Your flowers are a very personal part of your day, so make sure to choose a florist whose style you love and whom you're confident understands your wedding vision.

PERFECT AS A MINIATURE BRIDESMAID'S BOUQUET OR A HANDHELD CORSAGE FOR THE MOTHERS, THIS ARRANGEMENT BLENDS DEEP RED AND PURPLE BLOSSOMS WITH DARK GREEN HOLLY FOR A CLASSIC WINTER PALETTE.

OPPOSITE: IN NATURAL
SETTINGS, ADDITIONAL FLORALS
CAN BE USED TO MAKE THE
ALREADY BEAUTIFUL OUTDOOR
SETTINGS TRULY SPECTACULAR.
HERE, FULL FLORAL CEREMONY
ARRANGEMENTS IN EVERY
SHADE OF PURPLE ARE
COMPLEMENTED BY GARLANDS
OF FRAGRANT HERBS STREWN
ALONG THE FENCE, ALL SET OFF
WITH GLEAMING WHITE BOWS.

LEFT: THIS HAND-TIED
BOUQUET WAS NOT
CREATED TO BE AS ROUND
AS A TRADITIONAL NOSEGAY;
INSTEAD, MINIATURE PEACH
ROSES COMBINE WITH LARGER
WHITE, PINK, AND YELLOW
ROSES IN A CASUALLY
GATHERED FASHION.

CHAPTER ONE

WEDDING BLOOMS

PAGE 16: IS ANY FLOWER MORE PERFECT THAN A TULIP? A HAND-TIED WHITE CLUSTER WITH LONG GREEN STEMS MAKES THE IDEAL SPRING BRIDAL BOUQUET. IF YOU REALLY ADORE THESE BLOOMS, IT'S EASY TO PLAN YOUR ENTIRE FLORAL VISION AROUND TULIPS IN ALL SIZES AND COLORS.

OPPOSITE: THE CONTRAST OF WHITE ON GREEN MAKES A STUNNING DISPLAY, AS IN THIS BRIDAL BOUQUET OF ROSES, STEPHANOTIS, AND LILIES.

LEFT: THE WARM GLOW OF THE AFTERNOON SUN BRINGS OUT THE SOFT, CREAMY TONES OF PINK AND YELLOW IN THIS BILLOWING BOUQUET OF ROSES AND SWEET PEAS. THE FLOWERS' PASTEL COLOR SCHEME DOESN'T PRECISELY MATCH THE LAVENDER DECORATIONS AT THE RECEPTION, BUT COMPLEMENTS THEM PERFECTLY.

*T*he floral possibilities for your wedding are truly endless—the color combinations and the kinds of flowers available go on and on. Your florist will help you to narrow things down. For your first meeting with him or her, bring along pictures of arrangements you like from magazines and books, as well as a fabric swatch from your bridesmaids' dresses and, if you can, a photograph of your own dress. Also describe your ceremony and reception sites. Together, you and your florist will make the best choice of flowers to achieve the look you want on your wedding day.

OPPOSITE: SPRINGTIME BLOSSOMS—ROSES, TULIPS, AND CALLA LILIES—ARE SET OFF WITH SEEDED EUCALYPTUS FOR A FRESH, SEASONAL BOUQUET.

LEFT: MANY BRIDES OPT FOR DIFFERENT STYLES OF FLOWERS FOR EACH MEMBER OF THE BRIDAL PARTY. HERE, A COLOR-FUL NOSEGAY OF HOT-PINK CROCUSES, CREAMY PINK ROSES, AND FRAGRANT LILACS SEEMS QUITE BOLD NEXT TO SIMPLER BOUQUETS OF LILY OF THE VALLEY AND ROSES.

CLUSTERS OF INDIGO
HYDRANGEAS LOOK STUNNING
NESTLED WITH ANEMONES,
FREESIAS, SWEET PEAS, AND
OTHER LAVENDER–HUED
BLOOMS. THIS LUSH, BUCOLIC
ARRANGEMENT ALSO SMELLS
ABSOLUTELY HEAVENLY, WITH-
OUT BEING OVERPOWERING.

Roses, of course, have long been a favorite wedding bloom. But tulips, peonies, and lilies are close seconds, and orchids and other exotic flowers are popular as well. Vivid Gerbera daisies, textured mums, and sassy sunflowers are making appearances at many weddings today. Magnolias decorate countless Southern celebrations, and delicate, dainty stephanotis is probably the rose's favorite companion. Based on the color scheme you're thinking about and the setting of your wedding, your florist can suggest types of flowers that will give you the effect you desire. You can choose virtually any flowers you want, but take advantage of your florist's

(continued on page 29)

PAGE 23: WHETHER SPRINKLED ALONG THE AISLE BEFORE THE CEREMONY OR THROWN IN THE AIR AFTER IT, SHOWERS OF PRETTY, FRAGRANT ROSE PETALS ADD A SPECIAL TOUCH TO BOTH UNCONVENTIONAL AND TRADITIONAL WEDDINGS.

RIGHT: COLOR, COLOR, AND MORE COLOR—DON'T BE AFRAID TO BLEND BLOOMS OF ALL SHAPES, SIZES, AND SHADES TO CREATE UNIQUE ARRANGEMENTS. HERE, HUGE PINK PEONIES, THE DELICATE CUPS OF YELLOW TULIPS, VARIOUS RED BLOOMS AND BERRIES, AND EVEN A BLACK-PURPLE POPPY COMBINE EFFORTLESSLY INTO A BOUNTIFUL BOUQUET.

LEFT: TUCKED INTO RUSTIC BASKETS TIED WITH RAFFIA, BIG, BURSTING ZINNIAS IN DEEP, HOT HUES DECORATE THE PORCH FOR AN OUTDOOR SUMMER WEDDING. THE BEAUTY OF SUCH CASUAL ARRANGEMENTS IS THAT ANYTHING GOES— THE FRESHEST, BRIGHTEST FLOWERS YOU CAN FIND ARE JUST PERFECT.

RIGHT: MANY FLORISTS WILL
ALSO INCORPORATE CANDLES
INTO THEIR ARRANGEMENTS,
LIKE THESE FLOATING VOTIVES
SURROUNDED BY GREENERY.
THE COMBINATION OF LIGHT
AND COLOR CAN BE MAGICAL.

OPPOSITE: BIG, BURSTING
PEONIES ARE BEAUTIFULLY SET
OFF BY TINY WHITE BLOSSOMS
AND DAINTY GREENERY.
CONSIDER NOT JUST COLOR
BUT SHAPE AND SIZE OF THE
BLOOMS YOU DECIDE TO USE;
LIKE A PAINTING OR SCULP-
TURE, TEXTURE IS A CRITICAL
ASPECT OF FLORAL BOUQUETS.

PAGE 28: THE SMOOTH,
CURVED SHAPE OF CALLA LILIES
ECHOES THE FLOUNCE OF A
BRIDE'S GOWN. POPULAR
WHEN CARRIED AS SINGLE
STEMS DOWN THE AISLE,
AND EFFECTIVE WHEN USED
TO CREATE AN AMAZINGLY
RICH YET MINIMALIST
ARRANGEMENT, THESE
FLOWERS EXUDE BOUNTY,
BEAUTY, AND ROMANCE.

expertise in picking the most appropriate blooms for your day. For instance, you'll want to choose flowers that are hardy enough to withstand heat or cold—and to make it through your ceremony and reception without wilting or turning brown at the edges. Your florist will know to clip the stamens out of certain flowers, so that pollen doesn't get dusted on everything (like your wedding dress). Your florist will also know which types of flowers are most cost-effective; depending on when and where you are married, certain blooms will be "in season" or locally grown, so they

(continued on page 34)

BELOW: THE DELICATE PINK PETALS OF AN EXOTIC AMARYLLIS CREATE A STUNNING CONTRAST WHEN ARRANGED NEXT TO SMALLER, MORE TRADITIONAL, BUT NO LESS DELICATE BUNCHES OF WHITE HYDRANGEA.

RIGHT: BE ADVENTUROUS!
FOR A TRULY UNIQUE BOUQET,
TRY MIXING IN LEAVES, FRUITS,
OR EVEN VEGETABLES. THIS
BRIDESMAID'S SIMPLE DRESS
LETS THE UNUSUAL BOUQUET
(NOTE THE PEPPERS) REALLY
MAKE A STATEMENT.

OPPOSITE: DEEP, RICH HUES
AND UNUSUAL SHAPES CAN
COMBINE TO MAKE A STRIKING
BOUQUET. HERE, TRADITIONAL
RED ROSES ARE JUXTAPOSED
WITH BRIGHT YELLOW-AND-RED
PARROT TULIPS FOR AN
INTENSELY COLORED DISPLAY.

OPPOSITE: A SMALL NOSEGAY OF PINK AND WHITE TEA ROSES APPEARS ESPECIALLY PRECIOUS WHEN PAIRED WITH SEEDED EUCALYPTUS AND A DAZZLING RIBBON.

LEFT: A BILLOWING BOUQUET OF PINK PEONIES MAKES AN OLD-FASHIONED STATEMENT ON A GRAND SCALE.

RIGHT: THIS BOUQUET OF
SCARLET ROSES LOOKS SO
VELVETY SOFT, GUESTS WILL
WANT TO REACH OUT
AND TOUCH IT. RED IS A
WONDERFUL CHOICE IF YOU
WANT THE EFFECT OF A VIVID
SHADE BUT STILL WANT TO STAY
SLIGHTLY TRADITIONAL INSTEAD
OF OPTING FOR MORE MODERN
COLORS LIKE FUCHSIA,
TANGERINE, OR VIOLET.

OPPOSITE: FRAGRANT ROSES
AND STEPHANOTIS COMBINE
TO CREATE A STUNNING
GEOMETRIC ARRANGEMENT
IN LAYERS OF BRIDAL WHITE.

will not only be less expensive, they will look better. (You haven't seen too many
hardy tulips in the dead of winter, have you?) If you decide you can't live without
a certain flower and you'll do anything to get it, there's a chance that your florist
can get you out-of-season or "exotic" blooms by special ordering them from
another region or country—just remember that you will pay for this luxury.

In this chapter, you'll find examples of favorite wedding flowers, in various
colors and incarnations. Use them to start forming floral ideas for your wedding day.

CHAPTER TWO

FLOWERS

FOR THE

BRIDAL PARTY

PAGE 36: A BOUQUET OF
BUBBLEGUM-PINK ROSES
AND LAVENDER-HUED
GRAPE HYACINTH LOOKS
EVEN SWEETER WHEN TIED
WITH RIBBONS ADORNED WITH
TINY PURPLE BUTTERFLIES.

OPPOSITE: THE ROUND
SHAPE OF A TIGHTLY
GATHERED NOSEGAY IS
NOT AT ALL OVERDONE;
THE FRESH NATURAL BLOOMS
USED HAVE A WAY OF MAKING
EVEN A SCULPTED BOUQUET
LOOK LIKE THE FLORIST SIMPLY
CAME UPON IT THIS WAY.

LEFT: THE CREAMY
TEXTURES, SMOOTH HUES,
AND DISTINCTIVE SHAPES
OF ROSES AND CALLA LILIES
WORK WELL TOGETHER, AND
COMBINE TO MAKE A STUNNING
TRADITIONAL BOUQUET.

*T*he bride's bouquet is what dreams are made of. It's the centerpiece of your wedding flowers, the arrangement that inspires all the others. It should make a statement about you, and about your wedding. It should complement your gown. It should be made up of flowers that you adore. More than any other accessory, the bride's bouquet is truly her finishing touch.

You might choose a tightly clustered nosegay bursting with roses, hand-tied with beautiful ribbon, the green of the stems showing underneath—the most

(continued on page 45)

RIGHT: FLOWER GIRLS DON'T HAVE TO CARRY BASKETS—WHY NOT GIVE YOURS A SWEET LITTLE BOUQUET OF BRIGHT BLOOMS AND LITTLE BERRIES? THEY DON'T HAVE TO MATCH HER DRESS EXACTLY—HERE, THE LAVENDER BANDS OF THE FLOWER GIRL'S GOWN ARE PICKED UP IN THE DEEPER TONE OF THE PURPLE FRUITS TUCKED INTO THE FLOWERS.

OPPOSITE: PINK-TIPPED ROSE-BUDS NESTLED IN GREEN ADD A BIT OF COLOR TO THE BRIDE'S TRADITIONALLY ALL-WHITE ENSEMBLE AND SERVE AS A SURPRISE ELEMENT IN THIS BOUQUET OF WHITE ROSES. THE SHEER STRIPES ON THE BOUQUET'S RIBBON MIMIC THE ILLUSION SLEEVES OF HER GOWN.

LEFT: THE VIVID, TEXTURED ROSES AND SWEET PEAS IN THIS BOUQUET ARE STRIKING AGAINST THE PURE WHITE OF THE BRIDE'S GOWN, AND THEIR PETALS ECHO THE DETAIL OF HER FLORAL SILK BUSTLE. MORE AND MORE BRIDES ARE MOVING AWAY FROM TRADITIONAL PASTEL WEDDING FLOWERS, PREFERRING AN INTENSE SHOT OF COLOR INSTEAD.

RIGHT: UNLIKE ROUND
BOUQUETS, WHICH GATHER
BLOOMS INTO A TIGHT BALL
THAT COMPLETELY COVERS THE
PLASTIC BASE THAT SUPPORTS
THEM, HAND-TIED BOUQUETS
ALLOW THE FLOWER STEMS—
AND THE BRIDE'S HANDS—
TO SHOW. THE LONGER
SILHOUETTE OF A HAND-TIED
BOUQUET IS A PERFECT COM-
PLEMENT TO THE STREAMLINED
GOWNS FAVORED BY MANY
BRIDES TODAY.

popular bouquet style today. Or perhaps you want a huge, flowing bouquet of multiple flowers, with cascades of ivy. A composite bouquet looks like one huge flower—often a rose—but it's actually made by wiring together the petals from hundreds of perfect buds, and the effect is absolutely stunning. You could even choose to carry a single, gorgeous stem, perhaps a lily, rose, or orchid.

In addition to your personal preferences, the type of dress you choose to wear will help you decide what bouquet is right for you. A sleek, slim wedding dress, for example, calls for equally sophisticated and unfussy flowers. If you're wearing a full,

BELOW: THE SIMPLE SHEATH WORN BY THIS BRIDESMAID DEMANDS AN EQUALLY STYLISH BOUQUET. PINK CALLA LILIES GIVE THIS SMALL CALLA-AND-ROSE ARRANGEMENT A MODERN LOOK. NOTE THAT THE FLOWERS DON'T EXACTLY MATCH HER SILVER GOWN BUT PLAY OFF THE COLOR BEAUTIFULLY.

RIGHT: A BRIDE DOESN'T HAVE TO CARRY A BOUQUET FULL OF LARGE, HEAVY FLOWERS TO MAKE AN UNFORGETTABLE IMPRESSION. THE CONTRASTING TEXTURES IN THIS BOUQUET— PAPERY WHITE FREESIAS COMBINED WITH THE TINY, ROUNDED BELLS OF LILY-OF-THE-VALLEY—CREATE AN UNUSUAL YET CHARMING BOUQUET.

OPPOSITE: THIS BRIDE WEARS AN UNADORNED GOWN WITH A MODERN CUT, SHEER BACK DETAILS, AND ORNATE, JEWELED SPAGHETTI STRAPS; SHE'S SELECTED AN ASYMMETRICAL HEADPIECE AND FOREGONE A LONG VEIL. HER SMALL, VIVID BOUQUET ECHOES HER SLEEK, CLEAN STYLE.

lush ball gown with a long train and layers of lace, satin, tulle, and pearls, you can opt for a more generous and flowing bouquet as well, something with strands of greenery trailing elegantly down to the ground. Just be sure that your bouquet is easy to carry, and not too heavy—remember, you'll be holding it for much of the day, often for long stretches as you pose for photographs. If you're petite, be particularly careful; you don't want your bouquet to seem bigger than you are!

RIGHT: AN IRIDESCENT SILVER
RIBBON TIED IN A PLEASING
PATTERN PLAYS OFF THE BLUE
AND PURPLE HYDRANGEAS
IN THIS BOUQUET.

Whatever you choose for yourself—whatever flowers and colors you decide should be in your bouquet—the bridesmaids' arrangements will follow your lead. Their bouquets are smaller than the bride's, but they are often in the same shape or style, with similar or the same flowers and colors. And of course, their bouquets should match the shade of their dresses.

ABOVE: SPRING BOUQUETS ANY WEDDING PARTY WOULD DIE FOR—CLASSIC CLUSTERS OF WHITE, PEACH, PINK, AND LAVENDER ROSES AND SWEET PEAS. NOTE THE CHARMING SATIN BAND THAT GRACEFULLY COVERS THE STEMS, WITH ITS SMALL LAVENDER BOWS.

OPPOSITE: BOUTONNIERES DON'T HAVE TO BE COMPLICATED, BUT THAT DOESN'T MEAN SIMPLE CAN'T BE PRECIOUS. A SIMPLE ROSE, A TINY ORCHID, A BRIGHT YELLOW RANUNCULUS, OR A SPRIG OF LILY OF THE VALLEY CAN CREATE AN ULTRA-ELEGANT LOOK THAT COMPLEMENTS THE MOST STYLISH TUXEDO.

LEFT: THE CLASSIC FLOWER-GIRL ACCESSORY IS A BASKET OF ROSE PETALS ADORNED WITH SATIN BOWS. THE CUSTOM OF A CHILD TOSSING PETALS IN HER WAKE IS SAID TO BRING THE BRIDE AND HER GROOM BOUNTY, FERTILITY, AND FORTUNE IN THEIR NEW LIFE TOGETHER.

RIGHT: SOFT CORSAGES
OF PALE PEACH ROSES AND
SWEET GREEN HYDRANGEAS
ARE IDEAL GIFTS FOR HONORED
GUESTS, LIKE MOTHERS AND
GRANDMOTHERS, OR CAN
EVEN BE WORN BY YOUR
BRIDESMAIDS IN LIEU OF
CARRIED BOUQUETS.

OPPOSITE: TYING A FEW
CREAMY WHITE CALLA LILIES
WITH AN ELEGANT RIBBON
REALLY SHOWS OFF THEIR
ARCHITECTURAL QUALITY.
A BOUQUET LIKE THIS IS MOST
FLATTERING WHEN CARRIED
BY A TALL, SLENDER BRIDE.

The groom and groomsmen wear small lapel arrangements called bouton-nieres. The bloom chosen for these is one prominent in the bride's bouquet, such as a rose, gladiolus, or orchid. (This custom stems from the medieval tradition of a knight wearing his lady's colors to show his love for her.) The groom may wear a larger boutonniere, or one with multiple blooms or in a different color, so he'll stand out.

There are probably people outside your wedding party whom you'll want to present with personal flowers on your wedding day. Consider corsages for mothers and grandmothers—pin or wrist arrangements are available—or miniature bouquets for them to carry. Fathers and grandfathers should get boutonnieres. Any other honored guests—siblings, special aunts or other relatives, or close family friends you want to recognize—may also be presented with wedding-day blooms.

CHAPTER THREE

FLOWERS FOR YOUR GUESTS

PAGE 54: AN ENDLESS ROW OF PALE PINK ROSE BOUQUETS MAKES ANY OTHER EMBELLISHMENT ON THIS EXTRA-LONG RECEPTION TABLE IRRELEVANT. CLASSIC ARRANGEMENTS SUCH AS THESE GO FAR TO PROVE THAT SIMPLE CAN BE TRULY SPECTACULAR.

OPPOSITE: THIS STUNNING CENTERPIECE RESEMBLES A MINIATURE TREE WITH FLOWERS ARRANGED IN ITS BRANCHES. BLOOMS OF ALL SHAPES, SIZES, AND COLORS CREATE AN ECLECTIC, NATURAL LOOK. THE TALL "TRUNK" MAKES IT POSSIBLE FOR GUESTS TO SEE AND TALK TO EACH OTHER EASILY WHILE THEY ADMIRE THE BURST OF COLOR AND SCENT ABOVE.

LEFT: YOU DON'T HAVE TO CHOOSE ONE LARGE BOUQUET FOR EACH RECEPTION TABLE. THESE SMALL BUNCHES OF ROSES IN ALL SHADES OF PINK HAVE BEEN PLACED IN TINY SILVER VASES AND CLUSTERED WITH VOTIVES. A SPRINKLING OF ROSE PETALS ABOUT THE TABLE TIES THE SMALL ARRANGEMENTS TOGETHER.

Your centerpieces are well worth the time you take to imagine and create them, since your guests will be seated closely around these arrangements for your entire reception. No table is complete without a vase full of gorgeous blooms adorning its center. Perhaps more than any other decoration in the room, your centerpieces define your wedding style—its colors, its season, its degree of formality.

You might decide to coordinate your centerpieces with the personal flowers from the ceremony, using the same (or similar) flowers, greenery, and colors. You

OPPOSITE: VIVID PURPLE AND PINK ANEMONES STEAL THE SHOW IN THIS CASUAL AND NATURAL-LOOKING ARRANGEMENT. THE BLOOMS' INTENSE COLORS ARE FURTHER ACCENTUATED BY A TABLE DRESSED ENTIRELY IN WHITE.

LEFT: THESE GORGEOUS TWO-TONED ROSES ARE ARRANGED TOPIARY-STYLE IN A TERRA-COTTA POT DECORATED WITH MOSS. THE EFFECT HAS ALL THE CASUAL ELEGANCE OF AN ENGLISH COTTAGE GARDEN.

certainly want both types of arrangements to look as though they are from the same wedding, but concentrate on having your centerpieces set off the space where your reception will be. If your site is an intimate country inn, you'll likely want vases full of loosely arranged wildflowers; if your party will be in a grand ballroom, you might choose larger, more sculpted arrangements of white roses, stephanotis,

(continued on page 66)

RIGHT: DEEP PINK AND PEACH ROSES AND LAVENDER HYDRANGEAS IN A SILVER BOWL EMBODY THE IDEAL "NEW" CENTERPIECE LOOK. THE BOUQUET IS SHORT, FULL, AND ROUND, ITS CIRCULAR SHAPE ECHOING THE RECEPTION TABLE ITSELF. THE FLOWERS ARE TRADITIONAL, BUT THE VIVID SHADES GIVE THE ARRANGEMENT A MODERN TWIST.

OPPOSITE: THE PINK AND PEACH ROSES AND PEONIES IN THIS BOUQUET PICK UP THE FLORAL PATTERN OF THE PINK TABLE-CLOTH AS WELL AS THE DETAIL ON THE SILVER CHARGERS BENEATH EACH PLATE. THE PETALS SEEM TO GLISTEN IN THE SUNSHINE, JUST LIKE THE GLASSWARE.

FLOWERS AND CANDLES
COMBINE TO STUNNING
EFFECT IN THESE DELICATE
YET TOWERING CENTERPIECES.
IVY SLINKING DOWN THE
METAL STANDS CREATES
THE ILLUSION OF A LIVING
FLOWERING BUSH, AND PRETTY
VOTIVES ENCASED IN GLASS
SHINE ON TOP.

OPPOSITE: A SWEET IRON MESH
TEAPOT IS FILLED WITH VIVID
ROSES AND FLANKED BY TWO
SILVERY CANDLE LAMPS—THE
SILVER AND BLACK PLAY OFF
EACH OTHER BEAUTIFULLY.
EXTRA BUDS AND PETALS ON
THE TABLE, TUCKED AMONG
MINIATURE WHEELBARROW
FAVORS, MAKE THIS A
MEMORABLE STILL LIFE.

LEFT: SUNFLOWERS AREN'T
JUST GARDEN INHABITANTS
ANYMORE; THEY MAKE A BOLD
AND BOUNTIFUL STATEMENT
AT AN AUTUMN WEDDING.
HERE, THEY'RE BLENDED
WITH TEXTURED HYDRANGEAS
IN A TERRA-COTTA POT AND
SURROUNDED BY BUNCHES
OF JUICY PURPLE GRAPES.

RIGHT: A FLORAL TABLE CENTERPIECE DOESN'T HAVE TO BE HUGE IF YOU EMBELLISH THE LOOK WITH GLOWING LIGHT. HERE, A MODERATELY SIZED ARRANGEMENT OF YELLOW CYMBIDIUM ORCHIDS IN A STYLISH GLASS VASE IS ILLUMINATED BY A QUARTET OF COLUMN CANDLES.

and other traditional wedding blooms. An architecturally splendid room—perhaps in a historic mansion or an art gallery—calls for simple centerpieces with clean, sophisticated lines. Whatever your location, the flowers can pick up colors and shapes from the wallpaper, furniture, ceiling, and carpeting. Arrangements can also echo a holiday occasion—an Easter brunch is the perfect occasion to decorate with lilies or potted spring bulbs; a Christmas reception might mean poinsettias, or even miniature evergreens adorned with holly and tiny white lights.

Your centerpieces can be identical, with the same arrangement on every table and perhaps a larger arrangement on the head table, where the bride and

LEFT: LIGHT UP A ROMANTIC
EVENING WEDDING WITH
COUNTLESS CANDLES
REFLECTING OFF A SMALL,
SWEET CLUSTER OF ROSES.
THE YELLOW COLUMNS AND
VOTIVES PLAY UP THE GOLDEN
HUES OF THE FLOWERS TO
STUNNING EFFECT.

PAGE 68: SCARLET
CHRYSANTHEMUMS AND
DEEP RED ROSES ARE USED
WITH SPARSE GREENERY TO
CREATE A MONOCHROMATIC
BOUQUET IN DIFFERENT
SHADES OF THE SAME COLOR.
THE MULTIPLE DEPTHS OF
RED GIVE THE ARRANGEMENT
ADDED DIMENSION, AND THE
DEEP HUES COMPLEMENT A
MINIMALIST TABLE.

PAGE 69: TOPIARIES ARE A
NEW TREND IN CENTERPIECES.
THIS ONE IS DESIGNED AS
AN ENCHANTING ROSE BUSH,
WITH EXTRA BLOOMS PLANTED
IN THE GOLD-PAINTED VASE.
THE CHIFFON RIBBON DRAPED
AROUND THE TRUNK ECHOES
THE TABLE LINENS.

groom sit with their wedding party, their parents, or by themselves. Or choose several incarnations and place them around the room for an eclectic display. Try monochromatic arrangements, in which all the blooms are the same color, or perhaps select multiple shades of the same flower.

The kinds of bouquets you choose will affect what type of vases the flowers will sit in. Full, round bouquets of hearty flowers like roses and peonies generally look best in short, bubble-shaped vases. Long stems of orchids or lilies might necessitate sleeker, taller vases. Tie a ribbon around the neck of each vase for a beautiful finishing touch. And don't think only in terms of traditional vases—also consider baskets, urns, terra-cotta pots, even rustic buckets to hold your centerpiece flowers.

OPPOSITE: YOU DON'T HAVE TO CHOOSE JUST ONE OR TWO WEDDING COLORS AND DO ALL YOUR BLOOMS IN THOSE SHADES ALONE. THIS BOUNTIFUL BOUQUET INCLUDES A VARIETY OF FLOWERS—ROSES, SUNFLOWERS, HYDRANGEAS, MUMS—IN A RAINBOW OF COLORS.

LEFT: FOR A MODERN ROOM DONE IN DARK COLORS, OR ON A TABLE WITH RICHLY HUED DINNERWARE, CHOOSE CENTERPIECES WITH DEEP SHADES, LIKE THE MUTED PINKS AND GREENS OF THIS ARRANGEMENT. THE COLORS ARE ALSO IDEAL FOR ANY SUMMER- OR AUTUMN-THEMED WEDDING.

RIGHT: THIS IMAGINATIVE CENTERPIECE IS MADE UP OF FLOWERS AND FRUIT THAT HAVE SPECIAL MEANING FOR THE BRIDE AND GROOM. THE TROPHY-SHAPED ARRANGEMENT IS A LUSH CLUSTER OF DEEP-COLORED ROSES, CROCUSES, AND RANUNCULUS, TOPPED OFF WITH A PERFECT LIME. MOSS FILLS THE VASE ITSELF, AND ROSE PETALS ARE TUCKED INTO THE BASE FOR A FINISHING TOUCH.

OPPOSITE: NO GARDEN WEDDING WOULD BE COMPLETE WITHOUT A CHARMING CENTERPIECE SUCH AS THIS BRIGHT BOUQUET ARRANGED IN A WEATHERED WATERING CAN. YOUR FLORIST CAN DESIGN SOMETHING SIMILAR, OR YOU CAN CREATE YOUR OWN BOUQUETS WITH VIVID WILDFLOWERS IN WHIMSICAL CONTAINERS.

Think about the height of your centerpieces. Will guests across the table from one another have to crane their necks in order to converse? Remember fragrance as well; don't choose blooms whose scent might overpower the dinner.

Some couples choose to give the centerpieces away to a guest at each table as a thank-you gift. Others opt for multiple, smaller vases of flowers, enough for the entire table, so that the blooms can double as favors. Dried flowers or topiaries are also charming as centerpieces, and guests love to take them home. You can also augment floral centerpieces with additional decorations—candles, photographs, even bowls of fruit (for spring) or an arrangement of seasonal gourds (for fall), creating a true still-life display on each reception table.

CHAPTER FOUR

FLOWERS EVERYWHERE

PAGE 74: THE CLASSIC COMBINATION OF CANDLES AND FLOWERS GOES ONE STEP FURTHER. WROUGHT-IRON TRELLISES MADE TO BE DRESSED WITH FLOWERS ARE DRAPED WITH IVY AND WHITE BLOOMS, TOPPED WITH GLOWING HURRICANES, AND CONNECTED WITH GRACEFUL TULLE FOR AN ETHEREAL EFFECT.

OPPOSITE: FLOWERS ARE A SUBLIME CAKE GARNISH. A TRADITIONAL WHITE WEDDING CAKE, ALREADY DELICATELY GORGEOUS ON ITS OWN, BECOMES RAVISHING WITH PALE PEACH AND PINK ROSES DRAPED OVER EACH PRETTY TIER.

LEFT: A GARDEN WEDDING SETTING MAKES FLORAL DESIGN EASY—IT MAY ALREADY BE COMPLETELY DONE FOR YOU! HERE, THE STATUE IN A PRETTY FOUNTAIN ON THE GROUNDS GETS EXTRA EMBELLISHMENT WITH ARRANGEMENTS TUCKED AROUND IT, WHILE PETALS FLOAT IN THE WATER.

*P*erhaps your wedding site is a botanic garden, or a room so ornate and beautiful in and of itself that it doesn't need much additional decoration to make it a vision. You may well be able to simply choose stunning reception centerpieces and be done with it. But even if you're lucky enough to have found a spectacular setting, you should still consider whether there are other areas of your wedding that you'll want to embellish with flowers.

OPPOSITE: AN ALREADY IDYLLIC
OUTDOOR CEREMONY SITE IS
FURTHER ENHANCED WITH
FLOWERS AND PLANTS. AN
AISLE RUNNER STREWN WITH
PETALS LEADS TO A GORGEOUS
CANOPY CONSTRUCTED OF
TREE BRANCHES AND ADORNED
WITH HANGING GREENERY
AND PLUMP, LUSH ROSES. THE
FLANKING POTTED PLANTS
BRING IN THE SAME SHADES
AND BLOOMS.

LEFT: DON'T HESITATE
TO BRING FLOWERS INTO
YOUR CEREMONY IN NEW
AND UNEXPECTED WAYS.
A DECORATIVE CHAIR COVERED
IN GREENERY AND EXQUISITE
BLOOMS ADDS A CHARMING
AND WHIMSICAL TOUCH.

THESE CHERUBIC HEADS ARE
BEDECKED WITH LUSH WREATHS
OF GREEN HYDRANGEAS,
ECHOING THE FLUFFY CHIFFON
SASHES OF THEIR DRESSES.
LITTLE GIRLS LOVE FLOWERS IN
ALL FORMS, BUT THEIR HEARTS
WILL MELT FOR BLOOMS THEY
CAN ACTUALLY WEAR.

Let's start with the ceremony. Besides bouquets, boutonnieres, and corsages, are any other blooms needed? What about a little wreath for the flower girl to wear on her head? Or perhaps you'd like her to stroll down the aisle carrying a pomander (a flower-covered globe hanging from a pretty length of ribbon). Instead of a veil and headpiece, some brides choose to wear flowers in their hair—perhaps a wreath, blooms braided into the tresses, or even one large bloom behind one ear.

ALMOST ALL BRIDES CARRY FLOWERS, BUT MORE AND MORE ARE WEARING THEM, TOO. THIS FRESH FLORAL HEADPIECE WAS CREATED TO FURTHER BEAUTIFY THE BRIDE'S VEILING. YOU CAN WEAVE FLOWERS THROUGH LONG HAIR, TUCK A LARGE, EXOTIC BLOOM BEHIND ONE EAR, OR WEAR A FLORAL

ABOVE: UNCOMPLICATED
ARRANGEMENTS, ARTFULLY
PLACED, CAN MAKE AN ELEGANT
AND TASTEFUL STATEMENT.
HERE, PALE ROSES AND
NATURAL GREENERY SHINE
ON A RUSTIC TABLETOP

OPPOSITE: THE CASUAL RIOT
OF COLOR AND TEXTURE THAT
MAKES A COTTAGE GARDEN SO
APPEALING INSPIRED THIS LUSH
COUNTRY ARRANGEMENT.

Many houses of worship augment their building's architectural beauty with

flowers throughout the year, and especially during the holidays, but you may still

want one or two dramatic arrangements to adorn the area where you will exchange

your vows. (Be sure to ask your ceremony site whether there are any restrictions on

decorations before you start planning.) Consider traditional floral arrangements,

but also think about potted plants or greenery. If you're having a Jewish ceremony

complete with a huppah (the wedding canopy under which the couple is wed), you may want to decorate the top and sides of the canopy with blooms.

Some couples also decide to decorate the aisle, perhaps with strands of ivy or maybe just small flower arrangements at each pew, embellished with ribbon. You could even strew the aisle itself with petals, and then give each guest a sachet of those petals to toss as you leave the ceremony site as newlyweds.

OPPOSITE: AN ANTIQUE CAST-IRON URN OVERFLOWS WITH GORGEOUS BLOOMS AT AN OUTSIDE CEREMONY.

ABOVE: INSIDE, FLOWERS WORK ON A MORE INTIMATE SCALE, AS ROSES PROVIDE EACH GUEST WITH A BOTANICAL NAPKIN HOLDER.

RIGHT: FLOWERS CAN BE
USED TO DRESS UP THE SEATING
FOR CEREMONIES INSIDE AND
OUT. HERE, A SWEET SPRING
BOUQUET POPPED INTO AN
OLD METAL CAN MAKES A
CHARMING DECORATION,
AND FRESH SUNFLOWER HEADS
CHEERILY LINE THE AISLE.

OPPOSITE: EVERY FLOWER
GIRL DREAMS OF CARRYING
A BASKET BURSTING WITH
BRIGHT FLOWERS. SHE CAN
TOSS EACH FLOWER HEAD AS
SHE WALKS DOWN THE AISLE,
OR NOT—CHANCES ARE SHE
WON'T WANT TO PART WITH
SUCH GORGEOUS, AROMATIC
BLOOMS AS SUNFLOWERS
AND FREESIAS.

If your ceremony will not be in a church or synagogue, you'll certainly want to bedeck the area where you're actually married with floral arrangements. Some couples who marry outdoors choose to do so in a gazebo or under an arch lush with flowers.

At the reception site, consider whether you'll need additional arrangements for the head table, guest-book table, or cake table. Bridesmaids may place their bouquets in some of these places for the duration of the ceremony to help fill in— they can take the arrangements with them later as keepsakes. You may want to have your cake decorated with the same blooms that are in your bouquet or centerpieces; talk to your florist and your baker.

Be sure to have your florist visit the reception site with you soon after you decide to work together. Seeing the architecture of the space and the colors involved will help the florist to better assist you in selecting blooms that are well suited to the setting. Together you can decide whether you want to include floral arches over reception doors, wreaths on walls or windows, flowers adorning chandeliers or the backs of reception chairs—even flowers on the bride's gown.

OPPOSITE: THIS CAKE IS THE CENTERPIECE OF A TABLE LITERALLY BLANKETED WITH BLOOMS. THE PINK FLORAL FINIAL COMPOSED OF ROSES AND FREESIAS IS ECHOED IN MATCHING FLOWERS AT THE BASE, WHILE A FEW SPRIGS OF PURPLE BLOOMS PEEKING OUT FROM BENEATH THE TIERS GREET THE CARPET OF FLOWERS SURROUNDING THE CAKE.

LEFT: STYLISH BOWS DOMINATE THIS MINIMALIST WEDDING CAKE WITH ITS SMOOTH, EVEN FINISH, BUT FINIALS OF SMALL WHITE FLOWERS TOPPING BOTH TIERS GIVE IT THE GARNISH IT DESERVES WITHOUT OVERPOWERING THE CAREFULLY EXECUTED DESIGN.

RIGHT: THIS FULL BOUQUET OF PINK ROSES AND GREENS WOULD LOOK QUITE DIFFERENT IN A PLAIN GLASS VASE. A CHALICE-INSPIRED CAST IRON HOLDER LENDS EXTRA ELEGANCE TO THE ARRANGEMENT, MAKING IT LOOK POSITIVELY GRECIAN.

LEFT: A CASUALLY ARRANGED
GROUP OF PILLAR CANDLES
CAN BE ADORNED WITH ROSES
AND A SHIMMERING RIBBON
FOR AN ELEGANT YET SIMPLE
DECORATIVE TOUCH.

OPPOSITE: A CASCADE OF
LITTLE ROUND ROSES ALMOST
COVERS THIS TRADITIONAL
TIERED CAKE, MAKING IT
INTO SOMETHING COMPLETELY
ORIGINAL.

LEFT: A SMALL, SIMPLE SPRAY
OF FLOWERS GOES A LONG WAY
WHEN PAIRED WITH A CLASSIC,
WROUGHT-IRON CANDELABRA.
BY MIXING FLORAL AND
LIGHTING ELEMENTS, YOU
CAN CREATE A TRULY UNIQUE
ATMOSPHERE FOR BOTH THE
CEREMONY AND RECEPTION.

Belle Fleur

53 West 72nd Street

New York, NY 10023

Contact: Meredith Naga Perez

tel: (212) 579-4373

fax: (212) 579-4374

Cornucopia Flowers

28 West 27th Street

Suite 901

Contact: Dorothy Pfeiffer

tel: (212) 696-4323

fax: (212) 696-4123

Bridgehampton Florists

11 Main Street

Bridgehampton, NY 11932

Contact: Michael Grim

tel: (516) 537-7766

Perfect Parties by Robin

450 Seventh Avenue

Suite 3302

New York, NY 10123

Contact: Madeline Zeiberg

tel: (212) 563-2040

fax: (212) 563-2036

Christina P. Feufer Distinctive Floral Designs

143 West 29th Street

Suite 1

New York, NY 10001

tel: (212) 695-6680

Tapestry Bridal and Special Events Flowers

San Francisco, CA

By appointment

tel: (415) 550-1015

fax: (415) 550-8206

www.tapestryflowers.com

Principal photography ©Lyn Hughes: 1, 2, 3, 6, 9, 10, 12, 13, 14, 15, 16, 18, 20, 21, 22, 23, 24, 25, 26, 27, 28, 29, 31,
 33, 34, 35, 36, 38, 39, 40, 41, 42–43, 44, 45, 47, 48, 49, 50 all, 51, 52, 53, 54, 57, 59, 60, 65, 66, 67, 77, 78, 79,
 80, 81, 82, 85, 86, 87, 89, 90, 91, 92, 93

Courtesy Christina Pfeufer Distinctive Floral Designs, New York: 58, 62–63

©Dawn Photography: 88 (Flowers by Tapestry, San Francisco)

©Joshua Ets-Hokin: 46, 73, 83 (Flowers by Tapestry, San Francisco)

Courtesy Flowers by Tapestry, San Francisco: 30, 61, 72

©Glenn Jay Photography: 76 (Flowers by Tapestry, San Francisco)

©Jan Lundberg: 74 (Flowers by Tapestry, San Francisco)

©John Lyman: 19, 32

©Sarah Merians Photography & Company: 56, 69 (Perfect Parties by Robin, NY); 68, 70, 84 (Christina Pfeufer
 Distinctive Floral Designs, NY)

©Eric Schumacher: 71 (Flowers by Tapestry, San Francisco)

©Vera Photography: 64 (Flowers by Tapestry, San Francisco)

A B O U T   T H E   A U T H O R

Tracy Guth was an associate features editor at *BRIDE'S* magazine and the managing editor of The Knot (www.theknot.com) before striking out on her own as a freelance writer and editor specializing in wedding-related subjects. She has also written and edited for *Good Housekeeping*, *Seventeen*, Beatrice's Web Guide (www.bguide.com) and Astronet (www.astronet.com). Born and raised in Chicago, Tracy now lives and writes in New York City.